Adult
MAD LIBS™
World's Greatest Word Game

Kiss Me, I'm Single

By Roger Price and Leonard Stern

PSS!
PRICE STERN SLOAN

PRICE STERN SLOAN
Published by the Penguin Group
Penguin Group (USA) Inc., 375 Hudson Street, New York, New York 10014, USA
Penguin Group (Canada), 90 Eglinton Avenue East, Suite 700,
Toronto, Ontario M4P 2Y3, Canada
(a division of Pearson Penguin Canada Inc.)
Penguin Books Ltd., 80 Strand, London WC2R 0RL, England
Penguin Group Ireland, 25 St. Stephen's Green, Dublin 2, Ireland
(a division of Penguin Books Ltd.)
Penguin Group (Australia), 250 Camberwell Road, Camberwell, Victoria 3124, Australia
(a division of Pearson Australia Group Pty. Ltd.)
Penguin Books India Pvt. Ltd., 11 Community Centre,
Panchsheel Park, New Delhi—110 017, India
Penguin Group (NZ), 67 Apollo Drive, Rosedale, North Shore 0632, New Zealand
(a division of Pearson New Zealand Ltd.)
Penguin Books (South Africa) (Pty.) Ltd., 24 Sturdee Avenue,
Rosebank, Johannesburg 2196, South Africa

Penguin Books Ltd., Registered Offices:
80 Strand, London WC2R 0RL, England

Published by Price Stern Sloan,
a division of Penguin Group (USA) Inc.,
345 Hudson Street, New York, New York 10014.

ISBN 978-0-8431-3325-7

3 5 7 9 10 8 6 4 2

Adult

MAD LIBS™

INSTRUCTIONS

MAD LIBS® is a game for people who don't like games!
It can be played by one, two, three, four, or forty.

•RIDICULOUSLY SIMPLE DIRECTIONS

In this tablet you will find stories containing blank spaces where words
are left out. One player, the READER, selects one of these stories. The
READER does not tell anyone what the story is about. Instead, he/she asks
the other players, the WRITERS, to give him/her words. These words are
used to fill in the blank spaces in the story.

•TO PLAY

The READER asks each WRITER in turn to call out words—an adjective or
a noun or whatever the space calls for—and uses them to fill in the blank
spaces in the story. The result is a MAD LIBS® game.

When the READER then reads the completed MAD LIBS® game to the other
players, they will discover that they have written a story that is fantastic,
screamingly funny, shocking, silly, crazy, or just plain dumb—depending
upon which words each WRITER called out.

•EXAMPLE (*Before* and *After*)

"_____!" he said _____
        EXCLAMATION   ADVERB

as he jumped into his convertible _____ and
                                                    NOUN

drove off with his _____ wife.
                            ADJECTIVE

"_____*Ouch*_____!" he said _____*Stupidly*_____
        EXCLAMATION   ADVERB

as he jumped into his convertible _____*cat*_____ and
                                                    NOUN

drove off with his _____*brave*_____ wife.
                            ADJECTIVE

Adult
MAD LIBS™
QUICK REVIEW

In case you have forgotten what adjectives, adverbs, nouns, and verbs are, here is a quick review:

An ADJECTIVE describes something or somebody. *Lumpy, soft, ugly, messy,* and *short* are adjectives.

An ADVERB tells how something is done. It modifies a verb and usually ends in "ly." *Modestly, stupidly, greedily,* and *carefully* are adverbs.

A NOUN is the name of a person, place, or thing. *Sidewalk, umbrella, bridle, bathtub,* and *nose* are nouns.

A VERB is an action word. *Run, pitch, jump,* and *swim* are verbs. Put the verbs in past tense if the directions say PAST TENSE. *Ran, pitched, jumped,* and *swam* are verbs in the past tense.

When we ask for A PLACE, we mean any sort of place: a country or city *(Spain, Cleveland)* or a room *(bathroom, kitchen).*

An EXCLAMATION or SILLY WORD is any sort of funny sound, gasp, grunt, or outcry, like *Wow!, Ouch!, Whomp!, Ick!,* and *Gadzooks!*

When we ask for specific words, like a NUMBER, a COLOR, an ANIMAL, or a PART OF THE BODY, we mean a word that is one of those things, like *seven, blue, horse,* or *head.*

When we ask for a PLURAL, it means more than one. For example, *cat* pluralized is *cats.*

MAD LIBS® is fun to play with friends, but you can also play it by yourself! To begin with, DO NOT look at the story on the page below. Fill in the blanks on this page with the words called for. Then, using the words you have selected, fill in the blank spaces in the story.

Now you've created your own hilarious MAD LIBS® game!

LIVIN' LA VIDA SOLA

NOUN _____

PLURAL NOUN _____

VERB _____

ADJECTIVE _____

ADJECTIVE _____

TYPE OF LIQUID _____

ADJECTIVE _____

ADVERB _____

PART OF THE BODY_____

PERSON IN ROOM (FEMALE) _____

ADJECTIVE _____

NUMBER _____

VERB _____

ADJECTIVE _____

PART OF THE BODY_____

ADJECTIVE _____

ADJECTIVE _____

Adult MAD LIBS™
LIVIN' LA VIDA SOLA

Loving the single life? The perks are plenty! You are your own

_____. There's no need to check in with anyone
　　　　NOUN

when you and your _____ want to _____
　　　　　　　　　PLURAL NOUN　　　　　　　　　　VERB

after work. If you want to drop in for _____ hour at
　　　　　　　　　　　　　　　　ADJECTIVE

the local _____ bar and throw back a few glasses of
　　　　ADJECTIVE

_____, you can. And if you spot a/an _____
　TYPE OF LIQUID　　　　　　　　　　　　　　　　　ADJECTIVE

guy, you can flirt _____ with nary a care. Or, if you feel
　　　　　　ADVERB

like staying in, you can plop your _____ on the couch
　　　　　　　　　　　　PART OF THE BODY

and watch movies like *When Harry Met* _____ or
　　　　　　　　　　　　　　　PERSON IN ROOM (FEMALE)

_____ *Woman* for _____ hours straight. But
　ADJECTIVE　　　　　　　NUMBER

perhaps the best part of being single is that you don't need to come

up with an excuse every time you don't want to _____—
　　　　　　　　　　　　　　　　　VERB

like, "I'm too _____" or "My _____ hurts."
　　　　ADJECTIVE　　　　　　PART OF THE BODY

When you're single, you live your _____ life on your
　　　　　　　　　　　ADJECTIVE

terms—and it's absolutely _____!
　　　　　　　　ADJECTIVE

MAD LIBS® is fun to play with friends, but you can also play it by yourself! To begin with, DO NOT look at the story on the page below. Fill in the blanks on this page with the words called for. Then, using the words you have selected, fill in the blank spaces in the story.

Now you've created your own hilarious MAD LIBS® game!

MOST WANTED LIST

CELEBRITY (MALE) _____

NOUN _____

COLOR _____

PLURAL NOUN _____

ADJECTIVE _____

ADJECTIVE _____

ADJECTIVE _____

ANIMAL (PLURAL) _____

PLURAL NOUN _____

PLURAL NOUN _____

PLURAL NOUN _____

PLURAL NOUN _____

VERB ENDING IN "ING" _____

PLURAL NOUN _____

Is the perfect man too much to ask for? Never! At a minimum, he should:

1. Bear a striking resemblance to _____, making other
   CELEBRITY (MALE)

   women (and the occasional _____) turn _____
   NOUN   COLOR

   with envy.

2. Have a good enough job to shower you with sparkling

   _____—just because he can.
   PLURAL NOUN

3. Tell you every day how _____ you are and how
   ADJECTIVE

   _____ he is to have you.
   ADJECTIVE

4. Smile whenever he sees _____ children, fluffy little
   ADJECTIVE

   _____, or _____.
   ANIMAL (PLURAL)   PLURAL NOUN

5. Surprise you with little _____ under your pillow,
   PLURAL NOUN

   sweet love _____ taped to the mirror, or colorful
   PLURAL NOUN

   bouquets of _____ delivered to your office.
   PLURAL NOUN

6. Do his share of _____ around the house.
   VERB ENDING IN "ING"

7. Share his hopes, dreams, and _____ for a future with you!
   PLURAL NOUN

FROM ADULT MAD LIBS™: KISS ME, I'M SINGLE. Copyright © 2008 by Price Stern Sloan,
a division of Penguin Group (USA) Inc., 345 Hudson Street, New York, NY 10014.

MAD LIBS® is fun to play with friends, but you can also play it by yourself! To begin with, DO NOT look at the story on the page below. Fill in the blanks on this page with the words called for. Then, using the words you have selected, fill in the blank spaces in the story.

Now you've created your own hilarious MAD LIBS® game!

WHERE THE BOYS ARE

PLURAL NOUN _____

NOUN _____

ADJECTIVE _____

PLURAL NOUN _____

PLURAL NOUN _____

ADJECTIVE _____

NOUN _____

VERB _____

ADJECTIVE _____

NOUN _____

NOUN _____

NOUN _____

ANIMAL _____

PLURAL NOUN _____

ADJECTIVE _____

NOUN _____

NOUN _____

Adult MAD LIBS™
WHERE THE BOYS ARE

Finding the man of your _____ is like finding a/an
               PLURAL NOUN

_____ in a haystack. You can look in the usual places. At the
NOUN

grocery store, ask a tall, dark, and _____ guy to help you
                           ADJECTIVE

reach the canned _____ on the top shelf. When you're
            PLURAL NOUN

lifting _____ at the gym, ask a/an _____ guy to
     PLURAL NOUN   ADJECTIVE

watch your form. If you lock eyes with a cute _____
                                   NOUN

across a crowded nightclub, ask him to _____ on the dance
                           VERB

floor. But if you're really _____, you'll think outside the
               ADJECTIVE

_____. For example, roam through a/an _____
NOUN   NOUN

improvement store to find a man who knows how to wield a/an

_____. Take your pet _____ for a stroll
NOUN   ANIMAL

through the park. Volunteer to help save the _____.
                           PLURAL NOUN

Attend sporting events, and when you spot a/an _____
                           ADJECTIVE

hottie in the crowd, point your oversized foam _____
                           NOUN

directly at him and shout, "I'm your number-one _____!"
                           NOUN

Who knows? He may become yours, too!

FROM ADULT MAD LIBS™: KISS ME, I'M SINGLE. Copyright © 2008 by Price Stern Sloan,
a division of Penguin Group (USA) Inc., 345 Hudson Street, New York, NY 10014.

MAD LIBS® is fun to play with friends, but you can also play it by yourself! To begin with, DO NOT look at the story on the page below. Fill in the blanks on this page with the words called for. Then, using the words you have selected, fill in the blank spaces in the story.

Now you've created your own hilarious MAD LIBS® game!

FLIRT ALERT

ADJECTIVE _____

ADJECTIVE _____

NOUN _____

PART OF THE BODY (PLURAL) _____

ADJECTIVE _____

ADJECTIVE _____

ADVERB _____

ADJECTIVE _____

PART OF THE BODY _____

ADVERB _____

ADJECTIVE _____

EXCLAMATION _____

NOUN _____

PART OF THE BODY _____

PART OF THE BODY (PLURAL) _____

Adult MAD LIBS™
FLIRT ALERT

Flirting is a/an _____ art. Here are some tips for
                         ADJECTIVE

becoming a/an _____ master:
                    ADJECTIVE

- The eyes are the windows to the _____, so try
                                            NOUN

  batting your _____ or giving him a friendly,
               PART OF THE BODY (PLURAL)

  _____ wink. If you're feeling more daring, a sultry,
        ADJECTIVE

  _____ "come-hither" gaze is also _____ effective.
     ADJECTIVE   ADVERB

- If he says something _____, lightly touch his
                              ADJECTIVE

  _____ and laugh _____.
     PART OF THE BODY   ADVERB

- Appear interested in the _____ conversation by saying
                                ADJECTIVE

  things like, "Is that right?" or "I didn't know that!" or "_____!"
                                                              EXCLAMATION

- Make him feel like he's the most important _____
                                                      NOUN

  in the room. Maintain _____ contact and behave as
                        PART OF THE BODY

  though you only have _____ for him.
                       PART OF THE BODY (PLURAL)

MAD LIBS® is fun to play with friends, but you can also play it by yourself! To begin with, DO NOT look at the story on the page below. Fill in the blanks on this page with the words called for. Then, using the words you have selected, fill in the blank spaces in the story.

Now you've created your own hilarious MAD LIBS® game!

TACTFUL TURNDOWNS

NOUN _____

PLURAL NOUN _____

ADJECTIVE _____

NOUN _____

PLURAL NOUN _____

NOUN _____

ADVERB _____

ADJECTIVE _____

ADJECTIVE _____

PLURAL NOUN _____

NOUN _____

NOUN _____

NOUN _____

VERB _____

NOUN _____

NUMBER _____

A PLACE _____

Are you a/an _____ magnet? Do you attract all
NOUN

manner of geeks, jerks, and loser _____? Being the
PLURAL NOUN

_____-hearted person you are, you don't want to hurt
ADJECTIVE

the poor _____'s _____. But you also
NOUN   PLURAL NOUN

wouldn't date him if he was the last _____ on Earth.
NOUN

To let him down _____, try these tried-and-_____
ADVERB   ADJECTIVE

turndown lines:

• You're really _____, but we're better off just being
ADJECTIVE

_____.
PLURAL NOUN

• I already have a/an _____ with whom I want to
NOUN

spend the rest of my _____.
NOUN

• I just got out of a bad _____ and don't want to _____
NOUN   VERB

right now.

• I think of you more as a/an _____.
NOUN

If he doesn't get the hint after _____ minutes, just tell
NUMBER

him to give you a call—as soon as (the) _____ freezes over.
A PLACE

MAD LIBS® is fun to play with friends, but you can also play it by yourself! To begin with, DO NOT look at the story on the page below. Fill in the blanks on this page with the words called for. Then, using the words you have selected, fill in the blank spaces in the story.

Now you've created your own hilarious MAD LIBS® game!

GO AHEAD ... MAKE HIS DAY

PART OF THE BODY _____

CELEBRITY (MALE) _____

ADVERB _____

NOUN _____

ANIMAL _____

VERB _____

EXCLAMATION _____

PERSON IN ROOM _____

ADJECTIVE _____

PART OF THE BODY _____

ADJECTIVE _____

NOUN _____

VERB _____

ADJECTIVE _____

NOUN _____

VERB _____

NOUN _____

VERB _____

ADJECTIVE _____

Whenever you see him, your _____ starts to tingle.
PART OF THE BODY

_____, *eat your heart out,* you think _____.
CELEBRITY (MALE)   ADVERB

If only be would ask me out on a/an _____! But why
NOUN

wait? Take the _____ by the horns and ask him instead!
ANIMAL

Just _____ right up to him and say:
VERB

"_____! My name's _____. I couldn't
EXCLAMATION   PERSON IN ROOM

help but notice how incredibly _____ you are. Do
ADJECTIVE

you work out? I've been admiring your _____. It looks
PART OF THE BODY

so _____. Listen, I don't usually do this kind of thing,
ADJECTIVE

but can I buy you a/an _____? Or maybe we could go
NOUN

somewhere a little quieter and _____? The truth is—and
VERB

I hope this doesn't come across as too _____—I
ADJECTIVE

think there is a definite _____ between us. Anyway,
NOUN

I've got to _____ early tomorrow, so here's my phone
VERB

_____. _____ me sometime." You'll be
NOUN   VERB

amazed what a/an _____ dash of confidence can do!
ADJECTIVE

MAD LIBS® is fun to play with friends, but you can also play it by yourself! To begin with, DO NOT look at the story on the page below. Fill in the blanks on this page with the words called for. Then, using the words you have selected, fill in the blank spaces in the story.

Now you've created your own hilarious MAD LIBS® game!

COMPATIBILITY TEST

NOUN _____

ADVERB _____

ADJECTIVE _____

PLURAL NOUN _____

PLURAL NOUN _____

NOUN _____

PLURAL NOUN _____

VERB _____

NOUN _____

PLURAL NOUN _____

NOUN _____

NOUN _____

PLURAL NOUN _____

VERB _____

A PLACE _____

VERB ENDING IN "ING" _____

A PLACE _____

Is the new guy you've been dating really the yin to your _____?
NOUN

This test will determine if you two are truly destined to live

_____ ever after.
ADVERB

1. Does his idea of a romantic evening involve _____
ADJECTIVE

   music, dimly lit _____, and the two of you wearing
   PLURAL NOUN

   nothing but _____—and smiles?
   PLURAL NOUN

2. Does he believe that _____ doesn't grow on _____
   NOUN   PLURAL NOUN

   and that you have to _____ hard for the money?
   VERB

3. Does he remember to put the cap back on the _____,
   NOUN

   put dirty _____ in the _____ instead of all
   PLURAL NOUN   NOUN

   over the floor, and leave the toilet _____ down for you?
   NOUN

4. When he gets lost, does he stop to ask for _____ instead of
   PLURAL NOUN

   continuing to _____ until he winds up in (the) _____?
   VERB   A PLACE

If you answered mostly "no," he may not be your Prince

_____ after all. If you answered mostly "yes," you
VERB ENDING IN "ING"

two are a match made in (the) _____!
A PLACE

MAD LIBS® is fun to play with friends, but you can also play it by yourself! To begin with, DO NOT look at the story on the page below. Fill in the blanks on this page with the words called for. Then, using the words you have selected, fill in the blank spaces in the story.

Now you've created your own hilarious MAD LIBS® game!

DREAM DATE

NOUN _____

ADJECTIVE _____

NUMBER _____

NOUN _____

NOUN _____

NOUN _____

PLURAL NOUN _____

NOUN _____

PLURAL NOUN _____

VERB ENDING IN "ING" _____

ADVERB _____

NOUN _____

SILLY WORD _____

NOUN _____

PLURAL NOUN _____

NOUN _____

NOUN _____

A PLACE _____

MAD LIBS™
DREAM DATE

In a perfect _____, your _____ dates
                NOUN   ADJECTIVE

would always go a little something like this:

You slip into an outfit that makes you look like _____
                                                      NUMBER

bucks. Then, a/an _____ arrives, whisking you to an
                        NOUN

open-air restaurant atop a high-rise _____. A secluded
                                        NOUN

corner holds a/an _____ for two, accented with
                           NOUN

glowing _____ and a single, red _____.
        PLURAL NOUN   NOUN

_____ twinkle brightly in the sky, and from
    PLURAL NOUN

below, you can hear the sound of horns _____.
                                     VERB ENDING IN "ING"

_____, your date appears. "I've waited a whole _____
  ADVERB   NOUN

for you," he whispers. "You had me at '_____,'" you say.
                                 SILLY WORD

You share a passionate _____, and time seems to stop.
                        NOUN

Finally, after a meal of raw _____ and _____
                        PLURAL NOUN   NOUN

soup, it is time to part. "I must go," you say, blowing him a/an

_____,"but we'll always have (the) _____."
  NOUN   A PLACE

FROM ADULT MAD LIBS™: KISS ME, I'M SINGLE. Copyright © 2008 by Price Stern Sloan,
a division of Penguin Group (USA) Inc., 345 Hudson Street, New York, NY 10014.

MAD LIBS® is fun to play with friends, but you can also play it by yourself! To begin with, DO NOT look at the story on the page below. Fill in the blanks on this page with the words called for. Then, using the words you have selected, fill in the blank spaces in the story.

Now you've created your own hilarious MAD LIBS® game!

PERSUASIVE PICK-UP LINES, PART 1

NOUN _____

ARTICLE OF CLOTHING _____

ADJECTIVE _____

PART OF THE BODY _____

NOUN _____

NOUN _____

NOUN _____

NOUN _____

NOUN _____

VERB ENDING IN "ING" _____

NOUN _____

NOUN _____

ADJECTIVE _____

PART OF THE BODY _____

MAD LIBS™
PERSUASIVE PICK–UP LINES, PART 1

- Is that a/an _____ in your _____, or
  NOUN   ARTICLE OF CLOTHING

  are you just _____ to see me?
                ADJECTIVE

- I hope you know mouth-to-_____—because you
                            PART OF THE BODY

  just took my _____ away!
                NOUN

- If I said you had a beautiful _____, would you hold
                                NOUN

  it against me?

- Can I borrow your cell _____? I want to tell my
                         NOUN

  _____ I just met the _____ of my dreams.
   NOUN   NOUN

- Did you hear that? It's the sound of my heart _____.
                                                VERB ENDING IN "ING"

- If you were a laser _____, you'd be set on "stunning."
                      NOUN

- Is there a warrant out for your _____? Because it
                                  NOUN

  must be illegal to look that _____.
                               ADJECTIVE

- Are you from outer space? Your _____ is out of this
                                 PART OF THE BODY

  world!

FROM ADULT MAD LIBS™: KISS ME, I'M SINGLE. Copyright © 2008 by Price Stern Sloan,
a division of Penguin Group (USA) Inc., 345 Hudson Street, New York, NY 10014.

MAD LIBS® is fun to play with friends, but you can also play it by yourself! To begin with, DO NOT look at the story on the page below. Fill in the blanks on this page with the words called for. Then, using the words you have selected, fill in the blank spaces in the story.

Now you've created your own hilarious MAD LIBS® game!

PERSUASIVE PICK-UP LINES, PART 2

NOUN _____

VERB _____

NOUN _____

NOUN _____

ADJECTIVE _____

NOUN _____

NOUN _____

ARTICLE OF CLOTHING _____

A PLACE _____

VERB _____

PLURAL NOUN _____

PART OF THE BODY (PLURAL) _____

PLURAL NOUN _____

PLURAL NOUN _____

PLURAL NOUN _____

VERB _____

MAD LIBS™
PERSUASIVE PICK–UP LINES, PART 2

- Do you believe in _____ at first sight—or should I

  NOUN

  _____ past you again?

  VERB

- That's a very nice _____ you're wearing. It would

  NOUN

  look even better on my bedroom _____.

  NOUN

- What does it feel like to be the most _____

  ADJECTIVE

  _____ in the room?

  NOUN

- I lost my teddy _____. Can I cuddle with you instead?

  NOUN

- Can I check the tag on your _____ to see if you were

  ARTICLE OF CLOTHING

  made in (the) _____?

  A PLACE

- Did the sun come out, or did you just _____?

  VERB

- Can you empty your _____? I believe you've stolen my heart.

  PLURAL NOUN

- Are you a broom? Because you just swept me off my

  _____.

  PART OF THE BODY (PLURAL)

- Hey, baby, would you like some _____ with that shake?

  PLURAL NOUN

- I write poetry. "_____ are red. _____

  PLURAL NOUN   PLURAL NOUN

  are blue. How would you like me to _____ with you?"

  VERB

MAD LIBS® is fun to play with friends, but you can also play it by yourself! To begin with, DO NOT look at the story on the page below. Fill in the blanks on this page with the words called for. Then, using the words you have selected, fill in the blank spaces in the story.

Now you've created your own hilarious MAD LIBS® game!

BLIND DATES GONE BAD

ADJECTIVE _____

ADJECTIVE _____

VERB _____

PLURAL NOUN _____

PART OF THE BODY _____

VERB (PAST TENSE) _____

ADJECTIVE _____

PART OF THE BODY _____

PART OF THE BODY (PLURAL) _____

NOUN _____

ADJECTIVE _____

NOUN _____

NUMBER _____

NOUN _____

A PLACE _____

Thanks to the _____ matchmakers in your life, you've
ADJECTIVE

had your share of _____ blind dates. Luckily, you can
ADJECTIVE

now look back on these dating disasters and _____:
VERB

Mr. Immaturity: Preferred playing video _____ to
PLURAL NOUN

anything else. Laughed his _____ off whenever
PART OF THE BODY

he heard the word "joystick."

Mr. Metrosexual: Looked, smelled, and _____ better
VERB (PAST TENSE)

than you. Had a/an _____ habit of checking out
ADJECTIVE

his _____ in store windows.
PART OF THE BODY

Mr. Creepy: Kept his eyes on your _____ and
PART OF THE BODY (PLURAL)

his _____ in the gutter. On your first (and only)
NOUN

date, wore a/an _____ T-shirt proclaiming: "If this
ADJECTIVE

_____ is a-rockin', don't come a-knockin'."
NOUN

Mr. Arrogance: Repeatedly reminded you that he was president at a

Fortune _____ company, that he drove a/an _____,
NUMBER   NOUN

and that he had a vacation home in (the) _____.
A PLACE

FROM ADULT MAD LIBS™: KISS ME, I'M SINGLE. Copyright © 2008 by Price Stern Sloan,
a division of Penguin Group (USA) Inc., 345 Hudson Street, New York, NY 10014.

MAD LIBS® is fun to play with friends, but you can also play it by yourself! To begin with, DO NOT look at the story on the page below. Fill in the blanks on this page with the words called for. Then, using the words you have selected, fill in the blank spaces in the story.

Now you've created your own hilarious MAD LIBS® game!

THE PAMPERED SELF

ADVERB _____

PLURAL NOUN _____

NOUN _____

NOUN _____

TYPE OF LIQUID _____

NOUN _____

ANIMAL _____

NOUN _____

PART OF THE BODY_____

NOUN _____

ADJECTIVE _____

VERB _____

PLURAL NOUN _____

PLURAL NOUN _____

NUMBER _____

VERB ENDING IN "ING" _____

NOUN _____

NOUN _____

As a single gal, it's _____ acceptable to spend a little
ADVERB

time, and _____, spoiling yourself. Consider
PLURAL NOUN

a full-_____ massage at a day spa. Settle in
NOUN

for an evening with a steamy _____ and a hot cup
NOUN

of _____. Take the _____ off the
TYPE OF LIQUID   NOUN

hook and curl up like a/an _____ for an afternoon
ANIMAL

nap. Head to the beauty _____ and tell the
NOUN

stylist to try something that complements the shape of your

_____. Pay a visit to your favorite _____
PART OF THE BODY   NOUN

store and buy some _____ new things that will cause
ADJECTIVE

men to _____ in the street and follow you like lovesick
VERB

_____. Keep your mind and body the finely tuned
PLURAL NOUN

_____ they are by getting in at least _____
PLURAL NOUN   NUMBER

minutes of _____ every day. Really, it all comes down
VERB ENDING IN "ING"

to following the Golden _____: Treat yourself the way
NOUN

you'd want the perfect _____ to treat you.
NOUN

MAD LIBS® is fun to play with friends, but you can also play it by yourself! To begin with, DO NOT look at the story on the page below. Fill in the blanks on this page with the words called for. Then, using the words you have selected, fill in the blank spaces in the story.

Now you've created your own hilarious MAD LIBS® game!

YOU KNOW HE'S MR. WRONG WHEN . . .

PLURAL NOUN _____

VERB _____

ARTICLE OF CLOTHING (PLURAL) _____

NUMBER _____

PLURAL NOUN _____

PART OF THE BODY _____

ADJECTIVE _____

NOUN _____

NOUN _____

NOUN _____

ARTICLE OF CLOTHING (PLURAL) _____

PLURAL NOUN _____

NOUN _____

NEW YORK
IM 2 SXY
EMPIRE STATE

MAD LIBS™
YOU KNOW HE'S MR. WRONG
WHEN . . .

Adam

It might be hard to recognize Mr. Right, but you don't need to be hit

by a ton of _____ to spot Mr. Wrong! If he does any of
         PLURAL NOUN

the following, _____ in the other direction:
                  VERB

- He wears your _____.
                 ARTICLE OF CLOTHING (PLURAL)

- He tells you he has _____ active restraining _____
                       NUMBER   PLURAL NOUN

  against him.

- He repeatedly asks you to feel how muscular his _____ is.
                                                  PART OF THE BODY

- He offers to treat you to a/an _____ homemade
                                 ADJECTIVE

  dinner—then proceeds to thaw a frozen _____.
                                         NOUN

- He gives you a stuffed _____ for a gift—then tells
                         NOUN

  you how much his ex-_____ loved hers.
                      NOUN

- He asks you to foot the bill (again) because he left his wallet in his

  other _____.
        ARTICLE OF CLOTHING (PLURAL)

- He admits that, before he met you, he would hire paid

  _____ to go out with him.
  PLURAL NOUN

- He has a personalized license _____ that reads IM2SXY.
                                 NOUN

MAD LIBS® is fun to play with friends, but you can also play it by yourself! To begin with, DO NOT look at the story on the page below. Fill in the blanks on this page with the words called for. Then, using the words you have selected, fill in the blank spaces in the story.

Now you've created your own hilarious MAD LIBS® game!

DISHING ADVICE

NOUN _____

PLURAL NOUN _____

VERB ENDING IN "ING" _____

NOUN _____

NOUN _____

PLURAL NOUN _____

NOUN _____

NOUN _____

VERB ENDING IN "ING" _____

PART OF THE BODY _____

PLURAL NOUN _____

ADJECTIVE _____

ADJECTIVE _____

PLURAL NOUN _____

ADJECTIVE _____

PLURAL NOUN _____

NOUN _____

MAD LIBS™
DISHING ADVICE

It seems like everyone wants to help you find a good _____

NOUN

to settle down with. Your coworker suggests you hit on the good-

looking _____ around the office. Your neighbor

PLURAL NOUN

thinks that spending more time outside _____ in your

VERB ENDING IN "ING"

yard might help—like maybe mowing your _____ while

NOUN

wearing a two-piece _____. Your grandma, who's

NOUN

as old as the _____ but still sharp as a/an _____,

PLURAL NOUN   NOUN

warns you to behave like a proper young _____—

NOUN

which means no _____ until you are married. Your

VERB ENDING IN "ING"

girlfriends, on the other _____, encourage you to sow

PART OF THE BODY

your wild _____. Your mother claims you are too

PLURAL NOUN

_____ when it comes to men, and that if you're not

ADJECTIVE

_____, she'll end up without any grand-_____. Whew!

ADJECTIVE   PLURAL NOUN

You can appreciate that they just want you to be _____, but

ADJECTIVE

sometimes you wish they'd just mind their own _____.

PLURAL NOUN

You're happy playing the dating _____ on *your* terms!

NOUN

MAD LIBS® is fun to play with friends, but you can also play it by yourself! To begin with, DO NOT look at the story on the page below. Fill in the blanks on this page with the words called for. Then, using the words you have selected, fill in the blank spaces in the story.

Now you've created your own hilarious MAD LIBS® game!

YOUR ONLINE PROFILE

PERSON IN ROOM _____

ADJECTIVE _____

VERB _____

CELEBRITY (FEMALE) _____

PART OF THE BODY _____

NUMBER _____

ADJECTIVE _____

NOUN _____

PLURAL NOUN _____

NOUN _____

NOUN _____

NOUN _____

PLURAL NOUN _____

VERB _____

NOUN _____

ADJECTIVE _____

A PLACE _____

MAD LIBS™
YOUR ONLINE PROFILE

Welcome to the world of _____! I am the queen of
PERSON IN ROOM

my _____ universe, and I'm looking for a king to
ADJECTIVE

_____ alongside me.
VERB

Looks: Picture _____. Well, my _____
CELEBRITY (FEMALE)   PART OF THE BODY

resembles hers, but the similarities end there. That said, I would

still rate myself a solid _____.
NUMBER

Personality: People say my _____ smile lights up a/an
ADJECTIVE

_____. I get along well with all types of _____.
NOUN   PLURAL NOUN

And I never met a/an _____ I didn't like!
NOUN

Interests: I like _____ coladas and getting caught in
NOUN

the _____.
NOUN

Dislikes: _____-on-a-stick.
PLURAL NOUN

Accomplishments: I was once voted "Most Likely to _____."
VERB

In Summary: I rule with an iron _____. And I expect
NOUN

my king to obey all of my _____ desires. Together,
ADJECTIVE

we can take over (the) _____!
A PLACE

MAD LIBS® is fun to play with friends, but you can also play it by yourself! To begin with, DO NOT look at the story on the page below. Fill in the blanks on this page with the words called for. Then, using the words you have selected, fill in the blank spaces in the story.

Now you've created your own hilarious MAD LIBS® game!

BAD BREAKUPS

ADJECTIVE _____

NOUN _____

VERB ENDING IN "ING" _____

NOUN _____

PLURAL NOUN _____

NOUN _____

PART OF THE BODY _____

ARTICLE OF CLOTHING (PLURAL) _____

NOUN _____

VERB _____

NOUN _____

NOUN _____

VERB ENDING IN "ING" _____

NOUN _____

NOUN _____

NOUN _____

PART OF THE BODY _____

Breaking up is _____ to do. In fact, every time you

ADJECTIVE

give another _____ the boot, you swear you'll never

NOUN

date again—at least not *these* types:

Prince Cheating: You discover he's _____ with your

VERB ENDING IN "ING"

best _____! You scream, cry, and throw _____.

NOUN PLURAL NOUN

You call him every name in the _____. But the swift kick

NOUN

you deliver to his _____ is by far the most satisfying.

PART OF THE BODY

The Big Man: He wears the _____ in your

ARTICLE OF CLOTHING (PLURAL)

relationship, introducing you as "the little _____." As

NOUN

you _____ away for the last time, you remind him you're

VERB

an independent _____ with her own thoughts and

NOUN

feelings—and you think he's an insensitive _____.

NOUN

Chief Couch Potato: You've had it with him _____ all day

VERB ENDING IN "ING"

with a bag of _____ chips and the _____ control.

NOUN NOUN

You show him the _____—and let it smack him on the

NOUN

way out. Hey, it's one way to get his _____ in gear!

PART OF THE BODY

MAD LIBS® is fun to play with friends, but you can also play it by yourself! To begin with, DO NOT look at the story on the page below. Fill in the blanks on this page with the words called for. Then, using the words you have selected, fill in the blank spaces in the story.

Now you've created your own hilarious MAD LIBS® game!

WARNING SIGNS

NOUN _____

ADJECTIVE _____

VERB _____

PLURAL NOUN _____

NOUN _____

ADJECTIVE _____

ADJECTIVE _____

PLURAL NOUN _____

ADJECTIVE _____

ADJECTIVE _____

NOUN _____

VERB ENDING IN "ING" _____

ADJECTIVE _____

NOUN _____

MAD LIBS™
WARNING SIGNS

Dear Diary,

I've met the _____ of my dreams. Let me tell you all
NOUN

the _____ details. We always _____
ADJECTIVE   VERB

at my place because he says he doesn't want me to see the dirty

_____ in the sink or the clogged _____
PLURAL NOUN   NOUN

at his house. Isn't that thoughtful? And instead of taking me out to

_____ restaurants or to the movies (or anywhere in public,
ADJECTIVE

for that matter), we go on private, _____ picnics. He says
ADJECTIVE

he doesn't want to share me with anyone. It's so sweet! He doesn't

even want me talking to other _____ about us. He
PLURAL NOUN

says keeping our _____ relationship hush-hush makes
ADJECTIVE

it more _____. Isn't it romantic? He also won't let
ADJECTIVE

me call his house—he claims to be old-fashioned and thinks the

_____ should do the _____. Diary,
NOUN   VERB ENDING IN "ING"

doesn't he sound too _____ to be true? It just amazes
ADJECTIVE

me that another _____ hasn't married him already...
NOUN

FROM ADULT MAD LIBS™: KISS ME, I'M SINGLE. Copyright © 2008 by Price Stern Sloan,
a division of Penguin Group (USA) Inc., 345 Hudson Street, New York, NY 10014.

MAD LIBS® is fun to play with friends, but you can also play it by yourself! To begin with, DO NOT look at the story on the page below. Fill in the blanks on this page with the words called for. Then, using the words you have selected, fill in the blank spaces in the story.

Now you've created your own hilarious MAD LIBS® game!

HOW NOT TO LOSE A GUY IN TEN (OR TWO) DATES

NOUN _____

VERB ENDING IN "ING" _____

ANIMAL _____

NOUN _____

NOUN _____

ADJECTIVE _____

PLURAL NOUN _____

NUMBER _____

NOUN _____

NUMBER _____

PLURAL NOUN _____

ADJECTIVE _____

PLURAL NOUN _____

Adult

MAD LIBS™
HOW NOT TO LOSE A GUY IN
TEN (OR TWO) DATES

You really like the new _____ you're going on a first

                        NOUN

date with. To prevent him from _____ like a spooked

                              VERB ENDING IN "ING"

_____, here's what not to do on the first date:

    ANIMAL

- **Do not** wear a/an _____-encrusted tiara and comment that

                         NOUN

  you hope it matches your engagement _____ someday.

                                  NOUN

- **Do not** tell him how _____ you are about marriage.

                      ADJECTIVE

- **Do not** emphasize how excited you are about giving birth to lots

  of _____.

      PLURAL NOUN

- **Do not** leave him _____ messages on his answering

                     NUMBER

  _____—in the span of _____ minutes.

      NOUN   NUMBER

- **Do not** ask when he'd like to come home and meet your

  _____.

    PLURAL NOUN

Follow these _____ guidelines early on, and you

                ADJECTIVE

should be able to open up to him about your future _____

                                         PLURAL NOUN

together in no time!

MAD LIBS® is fun to play with friends, but you can also play it by yourself! To begin with, DO NOT look at the story on the page below. Fill in the blanks on this page with the words called for. Then, using the words you have selected, fill in the blank spaces in the story.

Now you've created your own hilarious MAD LIBS® game!

AFTER THE BREAKUP

PLURAL NOUN _____

ADJECTIVE _____

PLURAL NOUN _____

PLURAL NOUN _____

NOUN _____

NOUN _____

NOUN _____

ADJECTIVE _____

NOUN _____

ADVERB _____

NOUN _____

VERB ENDING IN "ING" _____

ADJECTIVE _____

NOUN _____

PLURAL NOUN _____

NOUN _____

NOUN _____

PLURAL NOUN _____

ANIMAL (PLURAL) _____

They say that time heals all _____. But a few

PLURAL NOUN

_____ rituals—for forgetting bad boys, bad memories,

ADJECTIVE

and bad _____—can also help. For example:

PLURAL NOUN

- Gather up all the _____ he's ever given you and toss

PLURAL NOUN

  them into the _____ -place. Add a lit _____

NOUN · NOUN

  and stand back.

- Write a/an _____ telling him what a big, _____

NOUN · ADJECTIVE

  _____ you think he is—then, instead of mailing it,

NOUN

  _____ toss it into the _____ can.

ADVERB · NOUN

- Head to the _____ mall and buy yourself something

VERB ENDING IN "ING"

  ridiculously _____. (It's a bonus if you're able to pay

ADJECTIVE

  for it with his credit _____.)

NOUN

- Put on a killer pair of _____ and your sexiest _____

PLURAL NOUN · NOUN

  and shamelessly flirt with everyone, from the guy who pumps your

  _____ to the fellow who bags your _____.

NOUN · PLURAL NOUN

  After all, there are plenty of _____ in the sea!

ANIMAL (PLURAL)

MAD LIBS® is fun to play with friends, but you can also play it by yourself! To begin with, DO NOT look at the story on the page below. Fill in the blanks on this page with the words called for. Then, using the words you have selected, fill in the blank spaces in the story.

Now you've created your own hilarious MAD LIBS® game!

GIRLS' NIGHT

NOUN _____

ADJECTIVE _____

PLURAL NOUN _____

ADJECTIVE _____

NOUN _____

TYPE OF LIQUID _____

PART OF THE BODY _____

NOUN _____

NOUN _____

VERB _____

NOUN _____

TYPE OF LIQUID _____

PART OF THE BODY _____

NOUN _____

A PLACE _____

NOUN _____

MAD LIBS™
GIRLS' NIGHT

Your _____ in shining armor may not have appeared yet, but
          NOUN

that doesn't mean you can't go out and have a/an _____
                                                     ADJECTIVE

time. Grab a group of your closest gal-_____ and paint
                                               PLURAL NOUN

the town _____! Head to the nearest _____-club
                ADJECTIVE   NOUN

and order up some shots of _____. Then get your
                                      TYPE OF LIQUID

_____ on the dance floor and shake what your
PART OF THE BODY

_____ gave you. If you spot a prime, Grade A beef-
     NOUN

_____ who's got some smooth moves, beckon him over
     NOUN

and _____ the night away. Just be careful. When last
          VERB

call arrives, he might ask you if you're interested in coming back to

his _____ for a hot cup of _____.
        NOUN   TYPE OF LIQUID

Before he gets the chance, excuse yourself to go powder your

_____. Then sneak out of there, jump in your
PART OF THE BODY

_____, and head back toward (the) _____.
     NOUN   A PLACE

You'll need a good night's _____ in order to do it all
                               NOUN

again tomorrow!

MAD LIBS® is fun to play with friends, but you can also play it by yourself! To begin with, DO NOT look at the story on the page below. Fill in the blanks on this page with the words called for. Then, using the words you have selected, fill in the blank spaces in the story.

Now you've created your own hilarious MAD LIBS® game!

SINGLES PLEDGE

ADVERB _____

VERB ENDING IN "ING" _____

NOUN _____

NOUN _____

NOUN _____

NOUN _____

NOUN _____

PART OF THE BODY _____

ADJECTIVE _____

PLURAL NOUN _____

ADJECTIVE _____

VERB _____

NOUN _____

PLURAL NOUN _____

VERB ENDING IN "ING" _____

PART OF THE BODY (PLURAL) _____

NOUN _____

PERSON IN ROOM _____

MAD LIBS™
SINGLES PLEDGE

"I do _____ swear that I am ready to commit to being
       ADVERB

single—for now. I know that _____ by myself is a/an
                 VERB ENDING IN "ING"

_____ of honor, not a/an _____ of shame. I am
  NOUN   NOUN

willing to wait as long as it takes to find a loving _____
                                        NOUN

who will appreciate me for the _____ I am, treat
                              NOUN

me like a/an _____, and not play games with my
                 NOUN

_____. Furthermore, I will not engage in
  PART OF THE BODY

_____ activities, like one-night _____,
   ADJECTIVE   PLURAL NOUN

that will only make me feel _____ afterward. I understand
                         ADJECTIVE

that it's better to be alone than to let someone _____
                                  VERB

all over me. I realize that focusing on myself right now will make me

a better _____ to someone else later. And I know that
     NOUN

when I see two elderly _____ _____ along
                   PLURAL NOUN   VERB ENDING IN "ING"

the sidewalk holding _____, it represents what I
                   PART OF THE BODY (PLURAL)

will have when I find the _____ of my life. My name is
                       NOUN

_____, and I am single—and fabulous!"
  PERSON IN ROOM

FROM ADULT MAD LIBS™: KISS ME, I'M SINGLE. Copyright © 2008 by Price Stern Sloan,
a division of Penguin Group (USA) Inc., 345 Hudson Street, New York, NY 10014.

This book is published by

PSS!

PRICE STERN SLOAN

**Look for these other fun Adult Mad Libs™ titles
wherever books are sold!**

Adult Mad Libs™: Advice for the Lovelorn

Adult Mad Libs™: Keepers and Losers

Adult Mad Libs™: Test Your Relationship I.Q.

Adult Mad Libs™: Party Girl

Adult Mad Libs™: Bachelorette Bash

Adult Mad Libs™: Dysfunctional Family Therapy

Adult Mad Libs™: Mama's Got a Brand-New (Diaper) Bag

Adult Mad Libs™: Who Moved My Cubicle?